SERIAL ENTREPRENEUR
FROM STARTUP TO SUCCESS

SERIAL ENTREPRENEUR

From Startup to Success

Elijah Desmond

Serial Entrepreneur From Startup to Success Copyright © 2018 by Elijah Desmond.

All rights reserved. No part of this publication may be reproduced, distributed, or transmitted in any form or by any means, including photocopying, recording, or other electronic or mechanical methods, without the prior written permission of the author, except in the case of brief quotations embodied in critical reviews and certain other noncommercial uses permitted by copyright law.

Jones Media Publishing
10645 N. Tatum Blvd. Ste. 200-166
Phoenix, AZ 85028
www.JonesMediaPublishing.com

DISCLAIMER:

The author strives to be as accurate and complete as possible in the creation of this book, notwithstanding the fact that the author does not warrant or represent at any time that the contents within are accurate due to the rapidly changing nature of the Internet.

While all attempts have been made to verify information provided in this publication, the Author and Publisher assume no responsibility and are not liable for errors, omissions, or contrary interpretation of the subject matter herein. The Author and Publisher hereby disclaim any liability, loss or damage incurred as a result of the application and utilization, whether directly or indirectly, of any information, suggestion, advice, or procedure in this book. Any perceived slights of specific persons, peoples, or organizations are unintentional.

In practical advice books, like anything else in life, there are no guarantees of income made. Readers are cautioned to rely on their own judgment about their individual circumstances to act accordingly. Readers are responsible for their own actions, choices, and results. This book is not intended for use as a source of legal, business, accounting or financial advice. All readers are advised to seek services of competent professionals in legal, business, accounting, and finance field.

Printed in the United States of America

Contents

Foreword 1

Introduction 5

Chapter 1: The #1 Risk in Life 7

Chapter 2: Defining Success 15

Chapter 3: Failure: Your Partner in Progress 23

Chapter 4: 5 Basic Things Your Business Needs to Survive ... 27

Chapter 5: Scale Up! 31

Chapter 6: Social Media: The New Google 41

Chapter 7: Partner vs. Investor 51

Chapter 8: It's About Them, Not You 57

Chapter 9: Network and Net Worth 63

Chapter 10: Mentorship: Your Ladder to Greatness 69

Chapter 11: A Few Million-Dollar Ideas 75

About the Author 79

Foreword

Elijah Desmond is one of those people you can't forget. He's all positive. And all energy.

Most entrepreneurs talk about big topics—like leading industries and improving lives—but few yield results that match their direction. We can all point to examples of people who hope for big things but lack progress. What I see from Elijah, however, is an ever-growing list of real accomplishments, each with a greater positive impact that builds upon the previous.

Over fifteen years, I have started and sold multiple seven-figure businesses in a variety of industries. As the CEO of Ideal Practices, I lead a nationwide consulting firm that works with dentists to open successful startup practices. I have become a best-selling author, have led teams of experts across the country, and have helped create some of the fastest-growth successes in my industry.

In my roles, I witness emerging needs for entrepreneurs, and one of these has become more impactful than any other. In short, today's most successful entrepreneurs focus on serving *others*. They are experts at helping *others* reach their aspirations. They lead *others* toward fulfillment. They relentlessly discover how to do this with each of their stakeholders. Customers. Partners. Vendors. Team members. Society.

Elijah is one of the best examples of someone who runs his businesses in this way. In just a handful of years, he has amassed the most influential people in his industry on his contact list. He has hundreds of sponsors ready to support his next projects. He has thousands of customers, many who literally follow him onto cruise ships. His online influence and communities are some of the largest in his industry. All this accomplished in just a couple short years.

How would you like your reputation to rise that fast in your industry? It can only happen in today's economy for entrepreneurs who excel at *serving others*. If you want to start or grow a privately owned business, you will need to learn what it means to *serve others* better than anyone else in your market. This is more important than profits. Some owners earn profits but neglect to elevate others along with their purpose. It is also more important than putting in hard work. Many do this but miss the exponential rewards reaped through leadership and inspiration.

The old paths of simple hard work and profits focus on self-serving goals only. The new emerging needs reveal the potential of focusing on others first. The best part about serving your stakeholders well is that you will grow more, help more, enjoy more, and even profit more.

Does it mean we can ignore profits? Of course not. That would lead to bankruptcy. Do these emerging needs for entrepreneurs mean things are easy? No. Neither does this approach mean that we cave to selfish demands from customers or employees.

The best part about these emerging methods of serving stakeholders is this: They make our work—and our lives—better. And this is where Elijah comes in. He makes the *lives* of stakeholders better by serving them with his positivity and his energy.

As an example, Elijah and I partnered recently in a business that brought the first-ever live continuing education course to dental professionals at no charge to any of its tens of thousands of viewers. In an industry thick with regulations, we achieved groundbreaking success with some crazy twists and turns (not the least of which was hosting the largest online live audience in the industry, immediately followed by my spending a night in a Mexican emergency room). Because we served an industry so thoroughly, other businesses now invest in our consulting services to implement this in their own industries.

What you will see in this book, and what I have come to respect firsthand, is a glimpse into the mind of a man who desires improvement and progress *for you*. He wants to serve you. You will see someone who leads with an empowering positivity. When obstacles and competing voices drag things down, Elijah refocuses people on the big picture that serves everyone best. He even manages to bring together the most unlikely collaborators to rally for the same goal. You will also see his unending energy. Beyond working long hours, this is an energy that attracts the best and inspires the best.

I encourage you to study this book. In it, you will get a peek into the mindset and ways of Elijah Desmond, as he implements the new emerging methods of entrepreneurs. Watch more than what he does; watch how he does it. If you do that, I assure you he will inspire you with his positivity and his energy.

From the moment you start reading this book, you won't mistake his style or his impact with those of anyone else you've encountered.

To you and your journey,

Jayme Amos
CEO, Ideal Practices
Dentistry's Elite Startup-Practice Consultants

Introduction

This book is largely inspired by my father. He is the man I had my early knowledge of entrepreneurship from, free of charge. I was so fortunate to have grown up under such influence. This encouraged me to start business early in life since I grew up knowing that entrepreneurship is the fastest and best path to achieving financial freedom and success. My father was also a very generous business owner who regarded lifting others as a responsibility.

The purpose for writing this book is to help as many entrepreneurs as possible who intend to start their own businesses and those that are already in business. I believe the journey is a lot easier when you have a blueprint of what it looks like – as I had from my father and mentors.

There are many conceptions and misconceptions out there that scare intending entrepreneurs about owning a business. Therefore, many prefer to stay in their comfort zone of paid employment. They believe having a job is far more secure than starting a business. Yes, there are a lot of risks in being an entrepreneur, so much uncertainty too. The idea of job security is a farce. There are no job securities anywhere, not in the United States. The best and surest path to living your dream life is entrepreneurship.

Think about it. Can you imagine the amount of money your skills and expertise make for the company you work for? You get a very small fraction of that amount. It was this realization that pushes a lot of people into starting their own businesses. You can too. Owning a successful business is not rocket science. What you need is a blueprint on how to go about it and, above all, the determination to succeed.

Through the ten chapters of this book I will share my tips and secrets that have helped me succeed as a serial entrepreneur. It usually is the most basic, fundamental principles that business owners refuse to apply that wreck their beautiful ideas. I hereby invite you to embark with me on this worthwhile journey of revealing those principles and more.

THE #1 RISK IN LIFE

Society is programmed against us from childhood. It is designed to stifle us and mold us to conform to certain societal norms. We are not allowed to develop at our own pace and on our own terms. We are programmed to behave in certain ways through the mechanism of constant caution, correction, punishment, and reward. We grow up in this constricted atmosphere, and by the time we become adults, we are already loyal conformists.

The number-one risk in life is being yourself. With every attempt to be yourself, you are likely to earn the badge of a deviant and a dissident. This is because such attempts, more often than not, result in breaking societal norms by doing the extraordinary and breaking limitations.

There are many people who influence our way of life, from early adolescence to adulthood. These people are those we spend most of our lives with. They influence our decisions at every point in time. It's important for an entrepreneur to identify these influencers and know how to manage their influences on you, especially as an adult. Let's discuss some of these life influencers and the extent of their influence on us.

Influencers

Parents

Your parents have peculiar character traits. That's who they are. Most times they were also programmed this way through influence from people around them as they were growing up. They have come to consider these character traits and lifestyle as the right and acceptable way of life. They in turn want to instill these traits in their children. Parents bring up their children to behave in certain ways that are in tandem with their own basic principal beliefs of life.

From the tender age of 1 to 5 our parents try to build us into the kind of ideal child they want us to be. They have a set image and perception of what the ideal child should be. When we come into this world, the mission commences. As a child, our parents determine the kind of toys we play with, the kind of toys they believe are good for us. They want us to play with a Tanker Truck when we want to play with Barbie.

An introverted parent is likely to frown upon their child who is showing traits of being extroverted. The parent feels this is not normal. They expect their child to be more moderate in his/her behavior and lifestyle. This leads to the parent trying to change their child's behavior through constant caution, correction, punishment, and reward mechanisms. Most parents want their children to grow up to be like them. They make deliberate efforts to bring up their children in ways that are in tandem with their principles and beliefs. We are all victims of this system.

Our parents tell us the kind of college we should attend and why we must attend college. Most of us were told a college degree is the ultimate key to success. Once you have a degree, get a job and start working for somebody. This is seen as a better financial security than being an entrepreneur. So, we go to college so that we can work for others, for the big corporations. Our education system has also been deliberately fashioned in this way.

Teachers

Teachers in school believe they know far better than their students. This is true. They also believe they know and understand their students better than the students know themselves. This is not always true. A teacher may want a child to participate in a certain sport because of talents and traits seen in the child. The child may not be interested in this sport although the teacher often succeeds by lording it over the child.

Since education is seen as very important, we hold our teachers in high regard. They are our role models. Their word is law. Many times, we accept their perspective on issues more than we do that of our parents. We sometimes copy their lifestyle in a bid to please them. No child wants to be the black sheep in the class. Teachers have great influence on us, an influence we sometimes carry into adulthood, our business, and approach to life.

Peers

Peer influence is more prominent during adolescence. Adolescence is the golden age of socialization and acculturation. During this period in life, we are being opened up to the world in its entirety. This is the period in which we begin to reveal our innermost traits and characteristic tendencies. The sense of independence that comes with this period makes us yearn for the freedom to be ourselves and do the things we want to do. We try to detach ourselves from our parents' and teachers' influence.

During adolescence, our peers are our greatest influencers. We want to do the things they are doing. They shape our opinion about many things. They help construct our beliefs and basic principles about life. We are in a constant struggle to fit in, to be accepted. We do a lot of things to be accepted, and we may lose ourselves in the process.

Life Partner and Family

Our partners become a great influence on us once we are married. In a broader sense, anybody we are in a romantic relationship with influences us in many ways. You are expected to be responsible to your spouse and children. Every element of your decision must have them in the picture. This influence is most times positive. However, it still goes a long way in determining how you live your life.

Many people are afraid to dump their paid employment and undertake entrepreneurship through fear of inability to care for their family and pay bills. When you are a family man or woman, you have great responsibility beyond yourself. This is why I strongly urge you to start your business before you get married. It is easier that way. Of course, as a married person, you can still plan your life in such a way that you are able to start your business. Just make sure you carry your family along.

Employer

To many people, their employer is their mini-god. Employers wield so much authority over their employees. As a matter of fact, they control the most productive parts of the employee's daily life. Employees spend their entire work week taking orders from their employers, doing their bidding, striving to please them. You can't imagine the level of psychological influence such a person and situation have on you. The word "employer" in this regard refers to a complex system of workplace control that involves the owner(s) of the company, superiors, company rules, workplace norms, and financial insecurity.

As an employee you are programmed to slave for the company and to regard it as more important than anything else in your life, including your family. You are made to understand that your happiness depends on the success and continued existence of the company. All these factors have a great influence on your psyche. You begin to see yourself in the light of your employment. This is a strong reason people are so afraid to lose their job. They cling on to that job through fear of the unknown.

Set Yourself Free

Freedom is the ability to act and live as you choose, without being subject to undue restraints or restrictions. The concept of freedom is largely attached to the ideas of time and money. The two are intertwined and rightly viewed as the most important resources of individual existence. What freedom means for an entrepreneur is spending your time as judiciously as you deem fit. You also have the ability to make money, as much as you desire, by spending your time on your own endeavor...YOUR business!

However, freedom does not come cheap, and there is nothing as absolute as freedom. Achieving financial freedom comes with a lot of time-consuming responsibility. What defines freedom for an entrepreneur is your ability to spend time working on your own terms and making money for yourself, not for others. This is one of the most important reasons people venture into entrepreneurship. They want to be free to do what they want, when they want, and how they want.

There are two forms of freedom: physical freedom and mental freedom. An entrepreneur needs both to survive. Being an employee can mean both physical bondage and mental bondage. Mental freedom is the more important of the two. Most people have physical freedom but lack mental freedom. Freedom of the mind is very important if you want to be successful as an entrepreneur.

Mental freedom is the ability to think outside the norm, the ability to create something from nothing. You must break yourself free from the stereotypes. You must refuse to see the boundaries. You must be willing to break the rules and take calculated risks. These are the qualities that define an entrepreneur. This is the entrepreneurial mindset. You must set yourself free. You must think like a creator; the work of an entrepreneur is to create solutions to problems. This is what is called value. It is this value that is converted to money. You have no business starting a business if it is not to create a solution to an identified problem. People only pay for solutions.

Discover and Be Yourself

People are constantly losing themselves out of fear of not being accepted. They want to fit into their society. As adults we are old enough to make decisions independent of others. However, we have already been engineered by society to think in certain ways and do things in specific ways.

The first step in your journey as an entrepreneur is discovering who you really are. You must break from society's definition of you and embark on a quest to discover your true self. An entrepreneur's first product is themselves. You must first discover, process, create, and package yourself.

You must first know who you are by understanding your passion, strengths, and weaknesses. Without a good understanding of these three cardinal elements of human composition, it is almost impossible to discover yourself and be just who you are meant to be. This is your treasure hunt. You must discover the treasure that is in you. From there everything else becomes easy, and you can navigate life with a better understanding and expectations.

Surround yourself with positive influences. Be around positive people. They will help you. The types of people we interact with go a long way in determining what we get out of life.

DEFINING SUCCESS

The concept of success is a fluid one. We all have different ideas of what constitutes success. Success can generally be defined as "the achievement of one's intentions." These intentions may come in different shapes and forms. Success is the sense of fulfillment we derive from having achieved our set goals and desires in a particular endeavor.

There are three main forms of success that affect an entrepreneur. They are Finance, Family, and Health. These three forms may be equally important to you, or they may vary in degree of importance. All three are tied into your business, and they interfere with one another either positively or negatively.

Understanding the 3 Main Forms of Success

Family

Family is the foundation of our lives. It is where everything truly begins. The first set of people we are introduced to when we start to gain consciousness of our immediate environment as kids are our family members. This is why these people become increasingly important to us as we grow up. It is this ingrained importance of the institution of the family that we carry on to our own marriage when we finally get married and start having kids. We see our spouse and kids as very important and central to our activities in life. They are thought of in our day-to-day decision making. Their happiness is the centerpiece of everything we do. We are ready to make necessary sacrifices to ensure that they are happy and comfortable.

This is what pushed me into becoming an entrepreneur — the desire to give my family a quality living standard. The desire to give my children the best education money can afford. The freedom to spend more time with my family. On the other hand, some people decide that entrepreneurship is not worth it, because it is time consuming, and entrepreneurs don't have enough time to spend with their family. These people prefer the 9-to-5 job that is time specific and, in their view, leaves enough time for family matters, with vacation benefits.

Finance

Money makes the world go 'round. Financial success is seen by many as the most important aspect in life. Most times when people refer to a person as successful it is because the person is financially wealthy. We need money to run our day-to-day existence. We need money to keep a family running and in good shape. Money is needed to give your children a better future. In fact, money is seen as central to human happiness.

Can you imagine a society without money? Without that force of motivation that gets things done and puts food on every table? Financial freedom is the number-one reason why most entrepreneurs strive to build businesses. I'll bet making more money is a major motivation for wanting to start a business of your own, the desire to make enough money to take care of your needs, to cater for your family and put smiles on their faces.

To achieve real financial success, you need to ask yourself what financial success means to you. For some people it means they can pay their bills and not live from paycheck to paycheck. For some other people it means that they can live in a mansion in affluence, while others just want to live a comfortable lifestyle.

Health

When we talk about health, we are talking about life itself. Without life there is no existence; without your existence there is no such thing as financial success or family success. You can only pursue other forms of success when you are in good health. Somebody who is ill, fighting for life, cannot think about making money. In fact, whatever money the person made before the illness may be spent to pay hospital bills. Then they are back to point zero.

Your well-being supersedes everything else. You cannot cater to your family when you are dead. Neither can you work for money if seriously ill. This is why you should place a premium on your health as an entrepreneur. Refusal to do so is putting all your dreams and aspirations in life in jeopardy. If you really want to achieve those goals, and you want to be as successful as you wish, your health should be a top priority.

The problem is that most entrepreneurs place little or no attention on their health. They skip periodic check-ups, refuse to get enough rest, don't make time for regular exercise. If you truly love your kids and spouse, you should take your health seriously. You don't want them standing by your sickbed in tears, traumatized. Neither do you want them standing by your grave looking into a bleak future for them without you.

What's Your Priority?

To find true happiness, It is important to have your definition of success clearly defined. True happiness lies in having a sense of fulfillment about life. That means you continually see yourself as achieving your own definition of success. This is what gives me great joy and a natural feeling of happiness.

Having a happy family is the definition of success for some people. They just want a spouse and kids to come home to. Such people may not find entrepreneurship attractive. Others want to be rich and famous. That's what gives them happiness. They want to be able to pursue their dreams without looking back. They are willing to remove any obstacle standing in their way. Such people will readily welcome a divorce whenever they feel their marriage is affecting their business or career. Absolute-freedom lovers cannot afford to have their freedom hampered by others, not even their family or their career or business. They just want to be free and have that liberty to do whatever pleases them at any time.

Life is a lot easier when you can set your priorities right. It is important for you to know the things that are most important to you and their order of importance. Do you value your family above all else? Is your freedom most important to you? Do you consider your ability to make money and become wealthy most important? What really makes you happy? What is that thing, that one thing, you are willing to sacrifice all other things for?

I want you to pick up a pen and paper now. Write down all those things you consider to be important to you in life, those things that give you joy. Then arrange them in order of importance, from the most important to the least important.

What Is Success to an Entrepreneur?

By now I'm sure you already understand the interrelatedness of the three forms of success to an entrepreneur. I call them the three cardinal aspects of an entrepreneur's success. Many erroneously think financial success should be what characterizes an entrepreneur's definition of success. You would be deceiving yourself by thinking making money is enough to earn you happiness and a sense of fulfillment in life. What is the essence of money without a happy family to spend it with? What use is money without good health to enjoy it with your family?

The end product of success is happiness. The reason we pursue success, whether as an entrepreneur or employee, is to achieve happiness in life. Financial success in and of itself does not guarantee happiness. Neither is family success possible without financial success. Both family success and financial success may just become a wish without good health.

Many shy away from entrepreneurship because they want to have enough time for their family. At the same time, it is important to build financial wealth so that you and your family can live the life of your dreams. If family is so important, isn't it equally important to make sure they get the best out of life?

You can only achieve ultimate success and happiness when you are able to marry success on the home front with success in business, without damaging either. This may seem to be a daunting task, but it is possible with effective time management.

Manage Your Time Effectively

It is already an established fact that the yearning for freedom is central to anybody's decision to become an entrepreneur. However, how that freedom is used to achieve true success depends on the entrepreneur's ability to successfully manage the number-one resource, which is time.

There must be a constant interaction between the desire to achieve financial success, family happiness, and the need to live a healthy life. It is this rapport that will help you balance the three in a way that will ensure a healthy interaction between them, through the instrument of effective time management. This is an entrepreneur's best path to success and happiness.

In the first two years of my marriage, I focused a lot on my financial success. I devoted most of my time to my businesses. I believed I needed to be financially successful first to have a happy family. So I was paying more attention to my businesses, and my family life began to suffer. However, at a point I came to a realization of which path I was taking. I saw the need to create a balance. I asked myself, If I have all the money in the world and there is no family to spend it with, what good is all that money?

Never tell yourself you should pursue financial success first and then come back to the family later. Or think that money is all that is needed to build a successful family. Your spouse and kids need you and your time as much as they need your money. Just like your business.

Weave Your Schedule

You should plan your day with the consideration of these three aspects of an entrepreneur's success. Your health, your family, and your business should feature in your everyday schedule. Let me tell you exactly what worked for me. I decided that my health is my business. It's part of my business to take care of my health. I make it a point to get to the gym a minimum of 3x a week. Often that is how I start my day. On Monday, I work from as early in the morning as I want until late in the day. It's a work day. I would not be available, from a family standpoint, unless it's an emergency. From Tuesday through Friday, either I work from as early as I want to until 1 pm and spend the rest of the day with my family, or else I start working at my business from 2 pm until late hours. On Saturday, I work until noon and spend the rest of the day with my family. Sunday is entirely family time. This is how I achieve massive family success. You should create a schedule that works for you.

Turn Vacation into 'Staycation'

Life is not meant to go on vacation once every year! Life is a vacation, so why not live in a place that is your "American dream" location? I was raised on a farm in Navarre, Ohio, where I quickly found out that farm living was not for me. Over the past nine years, I've lived in Ohio, Honolulu, and Las Vegas, finally settling down in Florida and calling Wellington, Florida, home!

Being mobile within your business can be very beneficial. I own five businesses, and at any given moment I could move anywhere in the country. When you do put roots down, ask yourself, Can I go on a vacation in my own backyard? Florida is a perfect example. Many people work their entire lives and then move to Florida to retire. They find a 55+ community with a clubhouse, pool, and daily activities available. My question to you is, Why wait until you are 55+? You need to plant your seeds in whatever environment you can see yourself in. I mastered this concept early in life, and I can tell you that if you are not happy where you live, you'll be wise to move to your dream location. If you want to build an empire, lay your bricks in your ideal vacation place.

Many businesses can be run from home, and you may be able to expense the portion you use as an office. Consult your accountant for the exact rules. With a mobile business, it is a lot easier to travel and also a lot easier to relocate. When moving to an area where you can't be mobile, you should make sure to do your research on the area! This is especially the case if you are depending on the people in your town as your primary consumers. Is there a need for your product? If you are not sure, it would make sense for you to do a survey prior to your relocation. The cost of living is another factor you need to consider.

You should also research the competition in your desired location. Competition can be good in some instances. When you are the first business in a market, introducing your product or service to the area may be difficult. If another company has already created a need, it's sometimes easier to come into that market. This is why McDonald's and Burger King are usually located beside each other. However, if the area is flooded with a variant of your product or service, you should research these companies and see if there is still a gap in the market.

Failure: Your Partner in Progress

One of the most important things you must take away from this book is the fact that you will fail. You will encounter failure at some point in your journey as you build your great business idea. The beautiful thing is that failure is part of the package. You must see failure not a full stop, but as a green light, saying Keep moving! No matter how beautiful your vision is, no matter how well thought out your plan, things will not always work in your favor.

I know following through is easier said than done. Yes, I know this to be true. But when you fail think of how far you have come, think of those who said it couldn't be done. Think of those waiting to see you fail. Stand up stronger and keep moving. Just when success is within sight, within grasp, within reality, people often give up.

Just Do It

I have mentored countless individuals who have earth-shattering ideas and are so excited about their ideas. As months go by, I check back with each individual to hear how they are progressing with their plan. Nearly 90% of the time I hear excuses, why they have not started. Many times they are just waiting for the right time to pursue their dream. Can I tell you this? There will never be a time in which you feel comfortable to carry through with your vision. Anything that's uncharted territory will not be comfortable, and you simply need to "Just DO IT" like the Nike slogan. There will never be a more comfortable time than now. Now is the best time to get started. Start Now!

Failure Means Keep Going

Encountering failure when you are just starting out may seem bad, but failure is not the end, it is the beginning. Look at it as you "bought the experience." The time and effort you put in are the price you paid to buy the experience. You need to pick yourself up, dust yourself off, and not necessarily start over, but MODIFY. Many times, things just need to be tweaked, not completely done away with. Whatever you decide to do, giving up should not be an option! Small failures are part of success. Remember the first time you rode a bike? You needed help, and eventually you rode that bike on your own. I can almost guarantee that you fell and scratched yourself at some point; however, did you stop trying to figure out how to ride? No. Climb up again and figure it out. You will eventually be able to ride the journey of life with no hands.

Discover the Magic Wand

When I started my second company, *Back to the Basics for Education, LLC*, in Hawaii I was consulting in four businesses. At a point I felt that I wanted more. I decided to move from Hawaii to a place where I could easily attract more businesses and chose Las Vegas. After settling there, I began to try all forms of marketing to attract new clients. I mean every type of marketing you could think of. I didn't win a single new client.

At one point I went out and purchased twenty cookie cakes that had this message in frosting: "I'm just trying to get my foot in the door." Each one had a baby shoe attached to it and my business card with a note saying, "Would you let me buy your lunch?" Can you guess how many responses I got from the twenty cookie cakes I delivered? ZERO! Not even a simple thank you. I concluded that this was the point where I had exhausted all my options, and it made sense to just give up.

My mother was the only one to whom I could relate my frustration at that time. I remember to this day how I rang her up and said "Mom, I have reached the end of the road. I don't know what else to do." Her next words were the game changer in my life. She said, "Well, I tell you what, the only way someone gets past me to my boss is if they come in with someone he already has a relationship with." BOOM! Just like that, by the next year I was consulting at twenty-three offices from Maui to Miami to Chicago and everything in between. I can never thank her enough for teaching me this life lesson.

You too must find that game changer. You must discover the magic wand that can open all doors for your business to grow and survive. It's good to have a great execution plan and work hard at achieving it, but, it's far better to know what works. Do not stop until you have discovered what works for your business!

Keep Your Vision on the Front Burner

How can you help yourself to stay persistent? First, you need to keep your vision at the front of your mind. Set up reminders of your vision in places you see every day, all day! My vision is always on the background of my computer screen or on sticky notes. Do whatever you can do to keep things in the NOW.

You should have long term-goals and short-term goals. Long-term goals are your final product, while your short-term goals are your long-term goals broken into attainable, realistic, time-bound bits. This is easier than trying to accomplish the long-term goal all at once. Remember, to build your house you must first build your rock-solid foundation and then erect the house on top of that foundation. Same thing applies to your business.

Some businesses need the walls completely broken down and a new foundation laid. This is not always a bad thing and in fact it could be the only option. Starting over on a clean slate and taking an entirely different approach could be a necessity. I would not consider this a failure, rather a new direction. Remember, you must keep going.

Make Yourself Accountable

Accountability always helps. Tell people you are close to attaining your goal and ensure that these people become your accountability partners. This is your free alarm clock, one you don't even need to plug in! Simply share your vision, and before you notice, you will be doing it. Why? Because you said you would.

5 Basic Things Your Business Needs to Survive

Many entrepreneurs have found themselves in unwarranted difficulties, caused by their own refusal to set the right foundation for their business. This chapter will discuss the five basic things you should have before starting your business. It is important that you lay this foundation to avoid problems in the future.

Choose a Business Name

Once you decide to start any business, you need to choose a business name. While this may seem easy, it could be one of the most difficult things to do! Don't stress yourself over it, for it will come. Make sure you are not in a hurry to reach a decision, because once you pick your name and start developing your business, you are stuck!

There are numerous ways to arrive at a good and unique business name. You can pick a word from an ancient language or a foreign language with a meaning that resonates with you and your client base. An example is the mobile app-based taxi company Uber. The word *uber* is a German word that means superb, non-comparable, or high-ranking. Another method is to use words, terms, or coinages that are familiar in your industry, for example, Microsoft. You can also decide to use an abbreviation of your own name or use your full name. This method is popular with the fashion industry. Such brands as Mary Kay, Michael Kors, and Tommy Hilfiger come to mind. You can also use words that describe the kind of service your business offers, Facebook and Smiles At Sea being ready examples.

Write out a list of all the names in your head. You want a name that will positively represent your business, a name that portrays the image you want your business to send. Image building and branding starts from the way you choose your business name. Start crossing out names on the list, from the least appealing until you arrive at a name you really find appropriate. As I said earlier, this process shouldn't be rushed. Take your time.

Before you reach the final decision on any name, make sure to check with your state to be certain the name is an available option. Then go to www.godaddy.com and see if that domain name is available or a variation of it. This way you don't find yourself at a crossroad later when you have to change your business name after you are in business and people already know you with the name.

Get Legal Protection

Now that you have a business name, you need to get some legal protection. Your next step is to seek legal advice. While this can be extremely expensive, I would recommend Ben Hilger from Legal Shield. He would give you the attention you need at an extremely affordable fee. You can have unlimited advice from an expert attorney for as low as $24.95 a month. His number is (808) 421-7672. Make sure you tell him you read the book!

The first thing you need to do now that you have an attorney is set up the type of business, for example, LLC, S-Corp, or C-Corp. This is what gives your business legal standing with the government and your clients/customers. It also separates your personal assets from your business if someone were to sue your business for whatever reason. It is extremely important to do this before you move forward with anything else. Once it's done, you should then apply for a Federal ID in the business world, or an EIN number. This is, in essence, your business's "social security number."

Acquire an NDA

Once you acquire legal protection you need to obtain an NDA, also known as a non-disclosure agreement. This is the final layer of protection you need for your interaction with other parties. You can obtain one of these for no charge with your legal membership with Ben. The NDA will essentially allow you to tell people your business ideas after they sign. This is very important when meeting investors, intending partners, etc. If you are going to take anything away from this chapter, take this: It's better to be safe than sorry. Unless you have an NDA, your friends and acquaintances can easily take your idea and run with it. Be safe with your business, so you don't become a statistic.

Set Up a Website

This is the internet age. You will be doing yourself and your business a great disservice if you don't have a functional website. No matter what your business is, you must have a website dedicated to it. Your website is your most effective medium for reaching the world easily. It is the easiest and fastest way to interact with potential customers. When people search the internet and can't find you or your business, you lose potential customer/clients!

You don't need to hire a big tech company or spend a large amount of money to have a beautiful, functional website. My websites are done by a company that I trust to pay attention to detail. The company is called OWL Computing. Visit my entrepreneur website, www.StartSuccessHere.com/NOW, to see this company's brilliant work. The company's contact is (616) 453-7505. While creating your website, OWL Computing can help you decide on your custom logo, from colors to font to style.

Online visibility includes more than a website. Social media is also important for online presence and marketing. We will discuss this in detail in Chapter Six.

Flyers and Business Cards

The last of the five basic things you need to get started are business cards and flyers. I use, and highly recommend, M13 for printing both your cards and flyers. They get things done fast with superb quality, and at a price you can't beat. Again, Christy Carrol Design is also a great company for design of your other materials, brochures, etc. Please do not cut corners by going cheap on your cards and flyers. They are what determines your first impression. Remember, "You get what you pay for."

SCALE UP!

Obstacles. They are the ultimate ingredients for growth. Without understanding how to use obstacles to grow, you will keep struggling and moving from frustration to frustration. I had to struggle before I understood how to grow from the obstacles I encountered.

Yes, you may be making a lot of money, getting more and more clients, and have the illusion of growth. Are you enjoying that money? You may find yourself struggling with fatigue, with happiness out of the picture. If so, you are putting too many unnecessary burdens on yourself.

Duplicate Yourself

I struggled for years trying to duplicate myself. The idea of finding another person with the same passion for my business that I had held me back. For me, this approach to growing my business was ineffective and counter-productive. I was looking for somebody who would be just like me! It took me five long years to realize there is nobody who can BE me. I am unique, just as YOU are unique.

Each of us is aunique, and we all possess unique skills, talents and abilities. The biggest problem an entrepreneur can create for himself or herself is to expect other people to be just like them. To expect other people to possess the same skill sets and have the same talents and abilities that we have is to wish for the impossible.

This expectation is why many startup entrepreneurs find it hard to scale up. They believe that for their business to be successful, other people working with them must be just like them. They find it hard to delegate important functions to their employees.

Some entrepreneurs, even though they may have several employees, cannot stay away from their business for a day. They must always be "on the ground" to do the most important things. Healthy growth cannot occur under such a circumstance. If you want to create a great business, you must learn the art of self-duplication correctly.

Self-duplication is key to the move from being self-employed to being a business owner. You are never a business owner until you have employees who can do the things you do and do them well. There are not many successful companies with a sole individual who does everything.

Apply the Magic of Specialization

You can't do it yourself.

I had a consulting business that became very successful. When I created it, I was charging $500 per month, and within three years I was charging $2500 per month. I was then consulting for three hours per month per client. That's roughly $150 to $800 per hour. It got to a point where I was consulting for 23 different companies. I had lots of money, but no time to spend the money. I discovered I was actually happier when I had fewer consulting clients. I realized you can have all the money in the world, but if you don't have the time to spend it, it's as good as useless. I had found it extremely difficult to go on vacation, to enjoy family time, or even have time for myself.

At that point I realized I needed to duplicate myself. I attempted to employ other people who could be like me. I hired ten different consultants. Here is the problem. They were great in their areas of expertise. However, some people were great at very specific things; others were not great at those specific things. Everybody had a specific talent to bring to the table, but no one had the kind of multitasking ability and talent that I had.

My dilemma? They all lacked the ability to sell. Essentially, I would have to close new business (sell), rather than deliver my consulting services. For 18 months I spent so much time training my team how to sell just like me that it became counter-productive. The more I trained them, the more I realized they didn't possess my same ability to sell and bring new businesses. It amounted to a huge waste of time and resources.

I was trying to duplicate myself as a sales person. The company didn't grow. The company shrank, because I was investing my time trying to make sales people out of people who couldn't or didn't want to sell. I was not selling, because I was too busy trying to make sellers out of my new employees. A lose-lose for sure.

A lot of entrepreneurs are faced with this problem early on. After hiring more people with the hope of expanding their business, the opposite happens. They become frustrated. They hold on to the idea that there are no competent hands to help them in their business. The problem lies in their improper implementation of the principle of self-duplication.

Instead, I decided to focus on something specific for each person, something the person was good at and enjoyed doing. Something he or she could do better. I allowed each person to specialize in something specific, namely, his or her area of expertise.

Develop Processes and Systems

The next important thing to do after self-duplication is to develop processes and systems. Anyone can easily pick up a manual or watch a video and do something important. Processes and systems need to be documented and consistent when you are onboarding a new employee. There should be a process and system in place for each area of your business, whether it's sales or customer support. When you are creating a business, you must make sure you document every single item. That way, when you are recruiting or training, the process is already in place. This alone will be one of the most significant things that help you grow your business.

Implementing self-duplication by trying to make people be like me didn't work. The moment I approached self-duplication by applying the magic of specialization (letting people work in their area of ability and expertise instead of trying to make them a jack of all trades) and developing a process and system, my business grew rapidly. This strategy may help ensure that the right people are put in place.

You should document your processes and systems of operation from the start of your business and keep improving them as your business grows. This shouldn't be too difficult if you have a good understanding of your business and hands-on experience. Simply create an outline; marketing to sales, sales to onboarding, onboarding to customer support, then your services. You can break this down into a bucket list of four to five items in an outline version, then take these four to five items and break each one down further. Doing so will give you the processes and systems you need.

This is absolutely something you can do on your own. You don't need to hire a professional or expend extra funds on it.

There is a very helpful software program called FLOWY that can help to ease the task.

Identify Your Strengths and Weaknesses

The biggest contrast that characterizes human existence is the possession of strengths and weaknesses. This is what underlines the fact that there is no superman... anywhere. Each of us is plagued with some deficiency that defines us. While our weaknesses amplify our deficiencies, our strengths sometimes make us appear superhuman. The way you manage your strengths and weaknesses is the true determinant of your success in life. It is extremely important that you know, understand, and master your strengths and weaknesses. Mastering your strengths will propel your business, while you can either outsource your weaknesses or work on self-improvement to turn them into strengths.

Maximize Your Strengths

Your strengths always find a way to surface and remind you they are there. They are those qualities and abilities you possess naturally, the things you find yourself doing almost effortlessly, with little or no training. Once you identify your strengths it's important also to work to improve yourself, acquiring the necessary skills to turn those innate abilities and potentials into kinetic abilities that work for your success. As the title of one of John Maxwell's books states, *Talent Is Never Enough*.

It is your responsibility to improve your strengths. For example, if you discover that you write effortlessly, attend writing classes to further improve that skill. Same with sales. If you are talented at sales, if you discover that you persuade people to buy things with little effort, attend trainings to further improve this skill. With the right knowledge you can easily take that ability to a whole new level. It is easier to work on improving your strengths than is working to improve your weaknesses.

Improve or Delegate Your Weaknesses

There are two basic ways to handle your weaknesses. You can either improve on them, or you can delegate to people who don't have the same weaknesses. You can attend classes, read books, and obtain materials online to help you strengthen those weaknesses. There are certain weaknesses we can easily improve on, while others are better delegated. You should identify those you can improve on and those you must delegate.

However, the easier route is to delegate. Doing this allows you to focus on your strengths. If you are not detail oriented, say, for example, you have little interest in anything to do with accounting, instead of expending time and energy learning to be an accountant, hire a competent accountant and delegate this area of your business to that person. Doing so allows you to focus on your areas of strength.

One of the reasons I have seen people fail in business is their refusal to delegate around their weaknesses. Instead of focusing on our strengths, we focus too much on our weaknesses. It is not bad to have weaknesses. Everyone has at least one. It's a normal human characteristic. You can't be good at everything. You shouldn't let your inability to do certain things make you feel bad about yourself.

Employ People with the Right Values

Your employees are not the owners of your company, and they may not care about your company as much as you do unless you empower them to do so. It is extremely important for you to empower them to feel that your business belongs to them too. This can be achieved by the way you treat them. Let your employees know they are important and valued. Let them know you appreciate their efforts and reward their smallest of successes. People feel a lot more attached when they know their efforts are recognized and appreciated. A company such as Google instills a sense of ownership into their employees by offering them shares in the company at a subsidized rate. When people know they also have something at stake, they are more likely to put all their effort into their work, because now they feel the company also belongs to them.

Above all things, you must ensure that you employ people with the right values. Nothing can replace that. You should make sure they possess the same core values as you, the kind of values that will give your company the right image you want. When your values conflict, working together becomes difficult. Value supersedes skills. Someone may have the required skill set and expertise, but if that person lacks the right values, he or she is not good for your business.

Outsource Marketing

I have seen countless businesses with amazing ideas and great products fail simply because the owners insisted on being their own marketers. Marketing may be your area of strength. If that's the situation, fine. If your strength is not marketing, you'll be wise to employ a marketer, or outsource your marketing to another company. It's also important to leave financial room for marketing. Make sure to include ample funds for marketing in your budget. Sales is the lifeblood of your business. You can't continue to be in business if you are not making sales. You cannot make sales if you are not marketing – and doing it right.

Construct a Vision with Goals and a Plan

You need to have a vision and a viable plan to grow your business. What do you want your company to look like in one year? Three years? Five years and beyond? Will you have five or ten employees? Are you looking at having a fifty-million-dollar business, or a hundred-million-dollar business? You should have a mental picture of what you want your company to grow into in a set period. Carefully create a plan that can help you actualize this vision. Once you have a plan, go to work on it!

One of my businesses is Smiles At Sea. We offer continuing education for dental, nursing, and EMS professionals on a cruise ship. My five-year plan is to charter an entire ship. I know that if I want to charter the entire ship, I need to attract a defined number of people to the cruise. The question then is, How do I get to that level? How do I get to that point where I can fill up an entire ship?

If you can state your vision clearly and break it down into small, attainable bites that define exactly how to get there, it will make your journey a lot easier. Your vision must come with a plan, a clear vision, and a well-crafted, simplified action plan. Your plan will help you achieve that vision in a timely manner.

Your vision is what you want your company to become. Your goals are the different things you want to achieve to get your business to that desired level. Your plans are the things you will do to achieve those goals. It's not good enough to have a vision. Neither is a plan of any value without specific, time-bound goals. You must break your vision down into small bites. Each of your action plans must have a deadline with specific goals to be achieved. You should hold yourself accountable to your deadlines and goals.

Make Bookkeeping a Priority

Financial record keeping is essential for growth and securing investments and future partnerships. If your business cannot afford to employ an accountant yet, you may want to hire a bookkeeper to help you keep a record of your expenses. Better still, with a basic knowledge of accounting you can keep your own records until you are able to hire a bookkeeper. Most importantly, you should know your status in terms of profit and loss and keep track of your income and expenditures.

You can hire a bookkeeper first and an accountant later. A bookkeeper is skilled in record keeping, tracking your numbers. Some bookkeepers can, however, do some of the work of an accountant. An accountant can do everything a bookkeeper does in addition to offering you financial guidance and planning, information on tax and tax breaks, and creating effective financial and organizational structure.

QuickBooks and Zero are two good software options for bookkeeping programs to help you keep good records. Initially either can be extremely overwhelming to use, but once you understand how to use it correctly, either should prove really helpful.

SOCIAL MEDIA: THE NEW GOOGLE

The internet is the biggest marketplace of the 21st century. It is the world's largest meeting point for buyers and sellers, and the melting pot for profound ideas. Businesses are moving away from traditional modes of marketing and embracing the power of the digital marketplace. Your business also needs to embrace this revolution if it is to survive and compete favorably in this new age.

Online Presence

You should have a strong presence online. The internet is your showcase, and social media is your magazine. Whatever the front page of a magazine can achieve for you and your business, social media can achieve more. Social media is the most cost effective and efficient way to market yourself and be heard. You can reach your target audience more easily on social media than on any other advertising platform. Social media also affords you the opportunity to build a community around your brand and establish a loyal customer following that can easily become your greatest asset at preaching the gospel of your business.

Be Yourself

Authenticity and originality are very important in crafting your image and reputation online. Do not make the mistake of painting yourself as a different person other than your real self. You will not be able to maintain the momentum. You are more comfortable and able to maintain whatever image and reputation you have when it is built on the real you.

In your quest to be yourself, you need to ask yourself one central question: Who am I? Do you project the kind of image you want your brand to have? If your lifestyle is not good enough for your brand's image, then you need to change. By change I do not mean you should create a false representation of yourself online. No, I mean you need to change your lifestyle. You need to change your character. You need to become a better you, one that is consistent with the kind of image and reputation you want your company to have.

Reputation Management

Reputation is everything. It is extremely important to understand, while you are building your business, that you are going to have an increasing number of eyes on you at all times. From a social media standpoint you must decide what your brand is going to be.

Online presence, especially via social media, has become the ultimate vehicle of reputation management. You must safeguard your company's online reputation. These days it is easy for disgruntled customers to destroy the reputation and image of a brand from the comfort of their own room. All that is needed is a smartphone, which almost every adult has these days, and an internet connection.

Facebook: Personal Account vs. Business Page

You can either decide to use your personal Facebook account and include people you do business with, or create a separate personal account you use for a business image. Personally, I prefer using my personal account and allowing people I do business with to see my personal life. It is easier for me to manage, instead of switching back and forth between my personal account and a personal account I use for business. However, this setup can prove to be counter-productive, depending on your lifestyle and the personal things you share on that account. A negative lifestyle can ruin your business image. You should also create a business page for your business on Facebook.

For the avoidance of doubt, let me explain how a personal account is different from a business page on Facebook. A Facebook page is a page that people can like and follow. Anybody who likes or follows your page can receive notification when you post. This page can be termed a business page, fan page, or public figure page. One disadvantage of a Facebook page is that the Facebook algorithm does not really favor posts on pages. That is, the number of people a page post can reach is very minimal compared to that of a personal account. For people to see what you post, you have to boost your posts. By boosting your post, I mean you pay for advertisement. This is a major way Facebook makes money. Then your post will become a sponsored post and therefore reaches more people. And there is a huge advantage in doing so. When you pay for Facebook to advertise your post, it affords you the opportunity to direct your post to your target audience through the demographic tools Facebook provides.

A personal Facebook account is the typical account meant for you to add friends. Whatever you post can be seen by people on your Friends list, without advertising. There is a twist to this, though. Facebook does not necessarily expose your post to everybody on your Friends list. This is why you can have 5,000 friends and only 200 people who see your post. Who sees what is tied to the engagements and reactions you can command on your posts. Facebook analyses the engagement and reactions you have on each post and uses them to reward or punish you on your post.

This is how it works. For instance, if you make a post today, it may be exposed to 200 people out of the 5,000 you have on your list. If most of those 200 people engage with your post by commenting and reacting, Facebook will consider your content interesting and beneficial to your audience and therefore expose your post to more people. On the other hand, if only few of the 200 people engage with your post, Facebook may consider your post as uninteresting to your audience and therefore reduce the number of people your post will reach. The key here is to make sure you create interesting posts that your audience will easily want to engage with, thereby increasing your reach.

Facebook only allows you to have 5,000 friends. However, after reaching 5,000 friends, you can have other people follow you. Your followers can also see those posts you make public, especially if they often engage with your posts through reactions and comments. You can also encourage people to just follow you or put you on See First. These options are available at the top of your Facebook profile when people open your profile.

You can open a Facebook page from your personal account and operate it from your personal account. I do not recommend opening two personal accounts. Doing so may affect the reputation of your brand when people see you operating two Facebook accounts.

Twitter and Instagram

Some people consider Twitter and Instagram more convenient to showcase their business, because of the way the two platforms are built. Twitter and Instagram pages are built on the system of followership. People can easily follow you and see all your posts on their timeline, and you can also follow others and always see their posts. Who sees what here is based on the relationship of the follower and the followed. Some brands find this system more interesting and convenient.

LinkedIn

LinkedIn is a professional form of social media. It is mainly for business owners and professionals to showcase themselves. As an entrepreneur, you should have a LinkedIn account. The site is very good for business networking and client acquisition.

If you are in the service economy, you can gain many clients on LinkedIn. Some prospective clients will look you up on LinkedIn. They want to learn about you, see what other people who have worked with you are saying about you, and know how professional and qualified you are.

Create Quality Content

The power of social media is very potent. It can make or mar you, depending on how you use it. When Myspace was very popular, there was this girl on it named Tila Tequila. She became very popular on the platform and had a large followership through her page, a single personal page. She became so popular on the platform that she went on to have a successful reality TV show. That's what social media can do for you.

You may have heard the saying, "Content is king." You need to have quality content to attract the right audience and create an addictive followership. Most people make the mistake of posting only about their business on their page. That's wrong. Your audience will get bored easily. To create a followership and a formidable community online, you need to post other things you know will interest and benefit your audience, aside from your business or product. This is the way to develop a strong followership online. Check out brands you like following. You will discover that it is not always the posts about their business that really get you addicted to their page. It's those extra values they offer.

Define Your Brand Approach

It is very important that you make a conscious effort to define what you want your approach to be and how you want people to perceive your brand. If you are a very serious person, stick to being serious. If you are very fun, stick to being fun. If you are very motivational, then most things you are posting should be motivational.

If you are a negative person, it might be a good idea for you to withhold the negativity on social media. Many people whose posts I see on a regular basis on social media are very negative. They vent. So, you must remember that when you are venting, you are venting to the entire social media world. This may destroy your reputation and people's perception about you and your brand.

Your Personal Life and Your Business Life

I know most people say you should separate your business from your personal life. Let me ask you a question. If you are doing business with anyone, would you like to see their family, know their background, and who they really are? I bet the answer is Yes. This is because it makes you feel more connected to the person and you feel more comfortable doing business with them. People buy from people they know, like, and trust.

That's how you should make your customers feel. That's how they want to feel. They would be more open to giving you their money and trust you more when they feel they know who you really are. People will feel like they know you and therefore will be more interested in doing business with you. However, if you are just starting your business and you feel your activities and posts on your page do not support a good image for your brand, you can delete that page and create another, still for you and your business.

Magazines and Social Media

Magazines used to be one of the best ways to get people to know about you and what you are doing. If you appeared on the front page of a popular magazine, more people got to know you and your business. So, in the past, business owners and entrepreneurs were very excited by the opportunity to grace the front page of a magazine.

Social media is the new magazine. With social media you can be on the front page of a magazine, so to speak, and with far greater reach. When you regularly post on social media, you put yourself on the front page of people's digital magazine. The viral nature of information on social media lets you accomplish in three years what used to take thirty.

Magazines put out a limited number of issues per year, while social media offers you limitless exposure. You can post every hour, every day. The more you post, the more followers and audience you gain, and the more people get to know about you and your business. In few months you can achieve what used to take a lifetime of appearing on the covers of magazines and submitting articles. For instance, if you have a Facebook group, different from a page, you can always post there and have people reading your posts every day. The more your community grows, the more people you can help.

Reality TV Shows and Facebook Live

At one point in the history of television, reality shows became very popular. A lot of them were aired, from *The Real Housewives of Orange County* to *Keeping up with the Kardashians*. People became increasingly interested in seeing how other people's daily lives looked. Viewers were excited by the idea of seeing their favorite stars in their natural state, creating a more familiar connection.

Facebook Live or Instagram Live gives you the ability to create this connection with your followers. The truth is, written language cannot replace the potent effect of spontaneous speech. People feel more connected to you when they can see you live, in your natural state, sharing ideas with them, talking to them about your business and products.

The biggest difference between TV reality shows and social media is the interactive mechanism, the instantaneous feedback and two-way communication. Your viewers can respond to your video by commenting. They can ask questions and you can answer instantly. The spontaneity creates a lot of magic. You should try it and do it often. You need it for your business, to build followership and a huge community for yourself and your brand.

Marketing on Social Media

Digital ads are essential for effectively marketing your business. Facebook and Google ads are very effective. Facebook advertising is blanket advertising. It's just like throwing a big fishing net into the large sea, hoping to get something back. You are going to be reaching a massive number of people. Google ads are targeted at a specific audience looking or searching for what you are advertising. Your goal is converting them into your customers.

Facebook ads are ads that you can use to boost to a very specific target audience. When you boost, you are sharing the post with people in a certain demographic. It could be women or men within a specific age bracket. You can also pick your zip code, state, and area of interest, i.e., people who are interested in certain things. Thus you can reach thousands of people within the specified demographic. You may experiment with your ads, using different keywords and switching the ads in order to achieve the best result.

It's very different with Google ads. For example, when somebody searches "massage therapist, New Mexico," what will pop up is a massage therapist ad; "lawn services in St. Louis" will pop up lawn services in St. Louis. Your business will appear on a specific search that relates to your business. A Google ad is a lot more expensive, but it is the most accurate way to reach your target customer. In this case you are not advertising to somebody who you hope might want your offer. You are advertising to somebody who is saying, "I want what you are offering!" It's as simple as that.

Your choice of ad may depend on your budget or financial strength. Facebook ads are by far more affordable. You would spend four to five times more on a Google ad than one on Facebook.

Partner vs. Investor

"I don't have enough money to do what I want with my vision." These words echo through my head as I remember creating my first business. Many times we find ourselves in this position: we need money to make our dreams realities.

The number-one cause of business failure is lack of capital. Many times people build on their amazing business ideas then fail through lack of money to market or perfect their business. Just imagine building the best product ever and not having the money to market it properly. If you have exhausted all your financial options, you may need to bring on a partner. Then the question becomes, Do I need a partner, or an investor?

Investor

An investor is somebody ready to invest their money in your business. Such a person will not necessarily be part of the day-to-day activities of the business. Their money works for them, and they have a share and, perhaps, a say in the company, depending on the percentage of their shares. Some investors will offer to render technical and managerial support. Make sure the role of your investors is well defined in writing! Many investors can become so domineering that they want to change your vision for your company. Just know that once an investor has a larger share in the company than yours, the business is no longer your own. The best title you can now have is founder or pioneer. Being CEO does not even matter. You can be removed at any time.

There are five major types of investors for startups. They are banks, peer-to-peer lenders, angel investors, venture capitalists, and personal investors. You may secure a bank loan to help you with your cost. The bank will require a convincing business plan, among other things. It is easier to secure a loan from a bank when you have an existing relationship with the bank. An angel investor is usually a successful entrepreneur who is interested in helping to fund startups. This person may buy a share in the company or lend you the money. Angel investors may also serve as mentors or advisers to you and your business.

Peer-to-peer lenders are online platforms that connect startup businesses with interested investors. Prosper is a website that offers peer-to-peer opportunities. You can list your startup project on the website to attract interested investors. Your credit worthiness comes into play here. The investor will request your credit history. Venture capitalists can be described as professional investors. They are often on the lookout for startups to invest in. This type of investor may be willing to put up all the money needed to start your business. However, they use their investment to secure equity capital or to buy a huge percentage of the company's shares.

Personal investors are friends and family. Many startups choose this route. You may borrow money from your friends and family to start your business. They may also decide to become your business partner. However, it is important to be very careful here, as it's not advisable to mix business and family relationships. Many people end up losing either or both. Whatever you do, make sure you have a documented agreement.

If at all possible, avoid letting any investor hold the majority share in your company. Decide what percentage of the company's shares you are offering to investors. You may decide to offer a maximum 40%. This 40% is what will be regarded as investor's share. The remaining 60% is exclusively for you as the founder. This way you ensure that you are always in control of your company and are still the major decision maker.

How to Find an Investor

Startup entrepreneurs are usually faced with the question of how to get investors. This is one of the reasons why networking and mentorship are very important. Through your network of friends in your industry, you may easily secure an investor simply by asking. You can also get an investor through your mentor, via their network. This is a benefit of having a mentor who is already successful in your industry or business generally.

You can source investors through such websites as LinkedIn, Quora, AngelList, and Microventures. Crowd Funding is another viable means of securing an investor. You can also raise capital to start your business through government funds for MSMEs in your country. You can also sign up for accelerator programs. Although they are highly competitive and time consuming, they may leave you better off and smiling. They are offered by NGO, investment funds, and business schools. Techstars and YCombinator are good examples. You can also put a call through to a big business school near you, as they usually have access to a wide network of investors.

Partner

A partner is somebody ready to offer expertise and money to join your business. A partner becomes co-owner with you. Partnerships are considered strategic because of the many benefits beyond money that they can offer your business. Sometimes a partner may not even bring money into the business, having only expertise to offer. Startups often take up to two years to turn a profit; it's not ideal, but it's a reality. Your partner could be a great asset to have on board, since he or she can work as an unpaid employee during this time. Such a situation will be more conducive to the business while it's in growth mode.

Bringing in money or not, a partner will also have a share in the company. Whatever the situation is, you need to decide carefully what percentage you are going to offer. If a partner is coming in at 50%, then communication is going to be the best thing to look for when determining if this is the right partner for you. Ask yourself, "Is that person's investment worth giving him or her half of everything? Is this person investing time, money, or both?" When making this decision, know that most people are more personally invested in something if they have committed more than their word and actually put money on the line. Make sure you spell out, in detail, the roles in the company and all details of your relationship in your operating agreement, which will be filed with the state.

What you both need to invest as partners should be basically the seed money to start the business and get it running. First, how much can you personally afford? This will help you know what you ask your partner to contribute. Before reaching this conclusion, make sure you have carefully created a budget that covers all of your startup costs, so as to avoid awkward situations in the future. Sometimes a person's expertise and time is more important than money. But someone who is financially vested has something to lose and thus will be more involved.

Consider the Pros and Cons

If not well managed, bringing a partner or investor into your business could be a bad decision. You may end up losing your company to others after years of labor. This is the fate such tech entrepreneurs as Steve Jobs and Elon Musk suffered early in their careers. It takes courage and a clear sense of purpose to survive such ordeals.

There are pros and cons to both having a partner and having an investor. When making this decision, do not be in a hurry, as the result may be a lifelong relationship. You need to make sure you choose the right person or persons. Take time to sit down with pencil and paper to list the pros and cons as a way to determine whether it makes sense to proceed.

Compatibility is Important

If you are accepting a partner, compatibility is the first thing you want to look for. The most important thing when going into business with a partner is your ability to work well together. The relationship is like a marriage, and if you are not on the same page it could be disastrous. Does each of you have a different expertise to bring to the table? This is an important question to ask yourself. Opposite personalities often complement and balance each other very well.

You should consider the person's character and attitude. You don't want to put up with someone whose behavior is largely upsetting to you. You won't be able to synergize with such a person, and that would definitely take a toll on your business. Are your temperaments compatible? If you don't know about temperaments yet, you should read a book on the subject. As an entrepreneur, you are going to be managing people, so you should understand the science of human behavior and know how to handle difficult people.

Ensure Proper Documentation

It would be foolish not to have your deed of partnership well documented, with clear roles assigned to each partner as well as the benefit each partner is entitled to. In starting a business there is nothing as valid as a written document, signed and witnessed by your legal adviser. Disagreements may arise with spoken agreements, but not with written ones. You can always refer to the document for clarification, particularly in a court case.

Make sure you are in constant consultation with your legal adviser during this process to be sure everything is done right. You may be outsmarted if you are not cautious enough. You should never rely solely on trust in a business situation. Trust may fail you, but a well-thought-out signed agreement will not. Your legal adviser will help you draft a well-thought-out document that all parties can sign.

It's About Them, Not You

John Mason, author of the book *Imitation is Limitation*, wrote, "People don't care how much you know until they know how much you care." In the same vein, people don't care about your product, or whatever benefit you say it will offer them, until they see that you care about them. Consumers want to interact with you first before interacting with your product or service. Don't make the mistake of putting the cart before the horse. You are the face of your product. People want to interact with that face before the product. Many times, when we want to sell to people, we are in a hurry to talk about the benefits of the product. Far too often you may try to sell to people when you don't even know what they need.

Establish Relationship

Business is more about relationship than about the sale. Yet often our preoccupation is to sell. Your first thought should be how you can help the person you approach. Be careful not to jump into strict business. The sale will follow naturally as an addendum when the relationship is first established. You need to place a premium on establishing relationship. When you approach a new business client, it is very important to get to know that person first, instead of immediately handing over your business card.

Establishing relationship first is a faster lane to making sales. When you get to know the person better, you understand his or her needs and are then better positioned to present your business or product in a way they can easily find beneficial and accept.

The mistake I made in business early on was thinking the signature on the contract was the most important thing. I was trying to grow fast and just get signatures. What I learned through experience was that if you are solely interested in getting signatures you are shooting yourself in the foot. The signature and the contract will not last long if there is no relationship. The relationship is more important than the business or product you are selling. A solid relationship will ensure that the person continues to buy from you.

Sell by Listening

I know you think that to sell a product you must do most of the talking. The truth is that you should talk less and listen more. Selling must be a two-way conversation, and the person who should be doing more of the talking is the consumer. Let them express themselves, or they are likely to be turned off. However, you can get them talking by asking thought-provoking questions. You can start by asking them about themselves or their business and how they feel your product or device can help them. In time, you will begin to realize what your consumers' needs are, and then you can ask further questions.

The same principle applies to your business meetings and pitching your business. While you may want to be formal, you must understand that you also need to be human. Being human is more important. Most times when you go into a meeting under pressure to make decisions or close a sale, the outcome is not ideal for either party. You achieve more through an exploratory conversation. That is not to say you shouldn't go with a well-planned outline. You should have an outline around which to weave your discussions.

Discover Their Pleasure Point

The cardinal goal of any service or product is to bring the consumer some form of pleasure. You need to know what makes someone happy if you want to bring them pleasure. The consumer's pleasure point is what they need, as opposed to what you may think they need. Often, we go into business meetings with our first instinct to give our ENTIRE business pitch. I caution you not to rush down this path, as your approach may not be the best approach. There are different angles you can take to earn the new business. But these would be difficult if you do not know that person's or that company's pleasure point. Knowing their pleasure point increases the odds of getting a yes to your offer.

Research prior to any business meeting is mandatory. Finding some things in common between you and the company or person you meet with can be the ice-breaker. Many times, if you can point out some facts about the consumer or tell them about themselves, it shows them you are highly interested in doing business with them.

Engaging in a two-way conversation is the most important thing you can do once you find their pleasure point. Once you find out your best approach, it is important to allow them to ask questions and not talk over them. When they ask questions, it means they are likely to be interested. Make sure you come prepared with all the answers you anticipate their asking.

Develop Your YES from Your NO

Many people give up when they hear the word "no" too many times. There are different approaches to battle the word *no*. I do not want you to battle or overcome that *no* and turn it into a *yes*, the way many would teach you to do. Rather than fight for a *yes*, I want to teach you to learn from your *no*. When you are turned down, try asking the million-dollar question: "Can you tell me why you said no and what would make you interested in my business/product/service?" The answers to this question are priceless. In fact, they can be better than a YES when building your business. It all depends on how you look at it. Honest answers will help you mold your responses in future situations.

If you constantly hear *no* and potential customers say your product or service is missing something, you need to fill that void. Everything doesn't necessarily come down to money. It comes down to value. If your value proposition is strong enough, the consumer will buy.

Within the first two to three years, you should know that you can't win them all. You must grow from your *no's* and constantly evolve. I promise you this: When you get your first *yes*, you will never get enough of it! Don't quit. You may just be one *no* away from striking gold on your next attempt. If you quit, you will never find out!

Inspire Brand Demand through Giving

If someone says your product or service should be free, you may think, *There's no way I'm doing a thing for free*. Well, if you consistently get that response, then that is exactly what your response needs to be. For example, if they want something for free, they may not really mean it. Instead, they just want a free sample. Give it to them!

The big picture in this situation is that you want to persuade them to try you out. Remember, if you have not established yourself yet, your task is to create a need, a demand. If your product or service is as good as you think, giving the customer

✦ It's About Them, Not You ✦

a sample to inspire brand demand is the best thing you can do. Go to the food court and you will see the restaurants doing this. Just remember, even high-end businesses such as BMW and Mercedes let you test-drive their product. Some even allow its use overnight. They know they are giving you a chance to experience their trusted brand, knowing in turn that you will fall in love with it and demand more. Another example is Mrs. Fields. She used to give her cookies away for free and everyone thought she was crazy. Now look at her. The cookies for which she created a massive brand demand are available in almost every food store.

NETWORK AND NET WORTH

The popular saying "Your network determines your net worth" is true. As an entrepreneur, you can hardly rise above the level of your business network. Business is done by people; it's a people affair. The more people you know, the better for your business. However, success is not just about knowing people. It's about knowing the people that matter.

The success of your business idea depends on the people you know. Imagine that you have a billion-dollar product or service but don't know the right people to invest in it with you. Imagine you have a few friends and a couple of business people, but that's all. Now let's take that same billion-dollar product or service and imagine that you know everyone in that industry.

If you can master networking, you can grow your business to any level. In this chapter we will discuss the different methods you can use to broaden your network and increase your net worth.

Associate with the KOLs

Major corporate organizations are investing millions of dollars into KOLs. You may be wondering what a KOL is. A KOL is a Key Opinion Leader in any specific industry. I will give you an example that almost everyone can relate to. LeBron James is a Key Opinion Leader in sports. This is why a company like Nike spends millions on him to represent their product. Another example is Tony Hawk, recognized as the extreme sport KING and skateboard idol. A company such as Monster Energy drink would sponsor him because he has a massive network and knows a lot of the right people. You can use the same model to grow your business. Remember, it's not what you know, it's who you know.

When growing your business, it makes sense to attend meetings where like-minded people gather. For example, if you are in dentistry, you should attend events where you can meet the movers and shakers of your industry. If your business is in marketing, you want to go where the KOLs in marketing are. You partner with these people who believe in your business for one MAJOR reason: they are influencers. It's important that you build a relationship with such people.

Instead of wasting $100,000 on direct mailers, you can take that $100,000 and invest in KOLs, whom you meet through networking. This is the contemporary way of marketing and branding. Many people hardly look at direct mailers anymore. It's an old way of marketing. Your direct mail is likely to end up in the trash can. Imagine sponsoring 100 speaking events throughout the country and paying that speaker $1,000 each time to simply endorse your business. As they are influencers in their profession, they carry more weight than a piece of mail. Studies show that less than 2% of direct mail gets the consumer to take action. Tell me which is more productive, being in front of 100 audiences by way of an influencer throughout the year, or being in a mailbox for one day hoping that 2% of people actually read what you sent them.

Attend Events

You remember that statement about being in the right place at the right time? It applies aptly to networking. Every industry has its movers and shakers, the influence wielders with the widest network in the industry. Entrepreneurs must attend industry events where they are able to meet these industry players. Apart from knowing these people, you should also work hard to increase your own influence to the point that you can join their ranks. You must start by associating yourself with them and learning from them. One of my businesses, Smiles At Sea, thrives on the wings of networking, and because of that, I am able to charge a premium for companies to be involved with it.

When you are networking, once you get someone's contact or preferably business card, email, or phone number, the next step is to build a relationship with the person. You can achieve this through follow-up. Send them an email about three days after your first meeting. Reintroduce yourself by stating what you stand for, whether it is the company you represent or simply you. If you don't hear back, you can send another email after a while, or call, if you have the phone number. Once you can establish this relationship, it becomes easy for you to draw on that contact whenever you need it. If you don't initially reach out, the other person won't remember you, as they meet so many people every day.

This is why you must have an excellent business card. Many times people will pass your card to their direct manager and even to the owner. Since the direct manager or owner did not meet you, your business card is what represents you. Whatever opinion they have about the quality of your business card will determine their opinion of you. If you did meet the decision makers, remember, they are also meeting many other people. Anything you can do to stand out will help them remember you. Your business card can do that.

Don't be quick to ask people for help when you first meet them. People at the top are inundated with requests for help from numerous people. But they seldom see people come out of the blue to offer them some form of help or appreciation. Don't join the bandwagon. Be different. They will appreciate you more if you approach them with a willingness to offer something, instead of taking from them. This will make you stand out. They will always remember you and always be willing to interact with you or respond to your emails.

Volunteer

Volunteering is a great way to network. Sometimes this can be hard because people are so stuck on their "worth." You never know whom you may meet or what relationship you may create when volunteering. You don't just volunteer because you want to be a good person, you volunteer because it can put you in front of the right people and build your network. You can volunteer to offer services associated with your industry, or decide to work with large corporations in your industry on certain projects for free. This way you will be able to meet industry players. Signing up for an unpaid internship early in your career is also another form of volunteering. By doing so, you can learn process and connect with people who may later be of great help to your business. It's advisable to intern at large or medium-size corporations. You have a lot to learn here.

Join Relevant Associations and Clubs

Professional associations and clubs have a huge concentration of active professionals. Being active in such organizations will help you increase your network and influence. Winning the fellowship of your industry association will improve your social standing. Through this, you can gain relevance in the industry. The people in your industry do in fact know what's currently happening and can help to further your agenda. You don't necessarily have to hold a position in the association before getting results through networking. Get involved now; stop sitting on the fence!

There are general, professional, and business clubs that you can join. Membership in many such clubs may be very expensive, but you can still find those that are affordable for you, then join others later when you have the financial muscle.

Build an Email List

Before the days of text messaging, email was our main source of communication other than picking up the phone. Emails most definitely have a place in the world of business, and it's important to grasp the concept of emails and following up. Many entrepreneurs are not maximizing the networking and marketing opportunities that email offers. We should get back to the basics and communicate via email efficiently.

It's important that you build an email list. Constant communication by sending regular emails keeps you in people's thoughts. You can decide to send emails to your list once every month or every week. Your emails should not just be about your company and product. To sustain your readers' attention, you should talk about other things that may be beneficial to them. For instance, if you are in the fashion industry, you can offer fashion tips. You should seek to create value with your content.

Ensure Prompt Response and Follow-up

Vacation or away alerts are your best friends! Prompt response is very important, and you can achieve that through an auto-responder. When people send you an email, they typically expect a response within 24 hours. Failure to do so is bad for you and your brand. If you are away for a few days, simply put the auto-responder on so that people expect your return but know you're on vacation. As a rule of thumb, I would suggest you set the auto-responder to indicate that you will return two days after your actual return. That way you have enough time to reply to all your emails. People will feel special that you responded (via the auto-responder) while away, instead of being irritated because you took so long to reply.

Life gets busy for most people, and many times all they need is a nudge or a friendly follow-up from you. They may forget to respond to your email or not remember the content of the email. Often they don't intentionally forget. You just need to remind them what your email was intended for. I recommend weekly, monthly, or quarterly follow-up so as not to constitute a nuisance for your readers.

Mentorship: Your Ladder to Greatness

I am a proud alumnus of Ohio State University and an advocate for college and higher education. I need to make that statement before I dive into this chapter, as it may appear that I'm advocating against college. I want you to understand that college is not always the only option. This accounts for the erroneous perspective most people have about life. A lot of people believe college education is the only path to financial success. This is not true. There are many paths to success in life other than college.

You can be successful and live the life of your dream without attending college. Don't ever allow yourself to be limited by your level of formal education. History boasts of many great people who had no college degree for one reason or another and still went on to get the best out of life. It all depends on your mindset. Greatness is never reserved for a particular section of society.

What Matters Is the Skill

I was 18 years old and seeking a big college life experience that encompassed dorm life, college football games, fraternity (Alpha Tau Omega), and parties. To be frank, I was going through a time in life where I was trying to discover my real self. Fortunately for me, I was awarded a scholarship to attend college at no cost, on the basis of my hard work in high school. For most of my friends, the story was not the same. Many left college with a degree but burdened by more than $100,000 in student loan debt.

I graduated as a dental hygienist, although I always told myself this was only temporary. However, it takes money to make money, and this was my start on a career path. I graduated with a bachelor's degree, while many of my friends graduated with an associate degree. When I got out of school I was surprised to discover that both levels of education received the exact same pay. I couldn't wrap my head around the logic behind this for a long time. As professionals, we were doing the exact same thing in a clinical setting, yet a person with a bachelor's degree and $100K debt was paid the same as the person with an associate degree and $25K in debt! It then dawned on me: it is not how you obtain your expertise, it is whether you have the expertise or not. That was when I discovered that I didn't actually need a higher degree to conquer my dream, especially if that dream was starting my own business.

Acquire Hands-on Experience

Whatever businesses you intend to venture into, you need hands-on experience in that industry to succeed. Do not go into any business until you are sure you know enough about it and are confident of achieving success. Nothing takes the place of field experience. You must know your industry. There is nothing as valuable as an understanding of the nitty-gritty of whatever you want to venture into. You can easily acquire this experience by attaching yourself to people and businesses that are already successful in the industry through mentorship and internship. Field expertise, to me, can sometimes be more valuable than your degree, especially when it comes down to finances

Climb on the Shoulders of Others

I encourage you, especially if you have more time than money, to follow someone who is already where you want to be. This will take a lot of your time; however, if you are not rich in money, then you are rich in time. Use that time to put yourself in a position where you can become rich in money. Eventually the time and money exchange will change to where you are rich in money and poor in time. The trick is finding the balance!

When you find yourself in a situation where you are debating going back to school or starting your business, remember that the majority of people do not care about the business owner's educational background. People care about one major thing: how good your product or service is. Think about it; do you really want to exchange your time and money for that degree? Would you rather just exchange your time and be mentored and save your money to start a business? I can tell you I earned my MBA through mentorship, and MBA to me is an acronym for Mentorship By Association!

Many of my peers think I got a degree in business. I did not. My early knowledge of business came from my hero, my dad, Addis Desmond II, who was named Businessman of the Year in Canton, Ohio, by the NAACP while I was in college. The rest of the credit goes to my mentors. I remember as I was growing up my dad was always pulling big stacks of cash from his pocket. He had multiple businesses, and he was his own boss, coupled with being extremely generous with his money. This was the foundation of my entrepreneurial mindset.

Many folks in business are so focused on their own success that they do not have time to mentor others. I call these people the rat-race merchants, and they are not the kind of people I surrounded myself with. I surrounded myself with successful people who were willing to share their success stories and mistakes. You should also surround yourself with such humans. They are waiting for you. Don't relent until you find them. Many of these people did attend college, but most of their time was spent in the field acquiring real-life experiences.

Find some mentors and latch onto them. They can be just as good as if not better than a college degree. Many entrepreneurs share their successes through books just like this one you are reading. You should read everything you can. Because I enjoy personal communication, I prefer direct mentorship. There are also audio books and YouTube videos about anything you can think of.

The Top Can Be Very Lonely

How could I have been like that? Yet these are the words that come to mind when I look back to my early years as an entrepreneur. Coming up in the business world, I will be honest; it was never about other people, it was just about me. Our big ambitions may work against us, just as much as they work for us. You can cause damage to yourself being so selfishly ambitious. You may feel you are doing the right thing, but you are doing it all wrong. Stop selling yourself and realize that you should be helping people too. Everything shouldn't be about what you stand to gain. There should be situations where you may not be benefitting but you are giving and helping others get through life's difficulties.

I realized in 2015 what giving was all about when I encountered Tracy Butler. This mentor of mine wanted me on her team; however, it was a ploy to help me. She taught me what life was like giving while still accomplishing your personal goals as a byproduct. When you have growing pains or are in a rough spot in business, suddenly all your issues disappear when you are helping others. You could be in the worst mood ever, and the moment you help, someone things change.

We all are trying to work our way up the ladder of life and are so focused on the very top. Let me tell you, the top is lonely. How many famous people do you know of who have committed suicide, overdosed, gone to jail, or are visibly unhappy? There are so many. On my way climbing the ladder of success I decided to take one hand off the ladder and reach back to help people climb up with me. It was scary to take my hand off the wheels of life at first. Once I did it a few times, I realized it wasn't that bad after all. In fact, it felt better than a personal achievement in life. It was my happy place and a success in and of itself. This encouraged me take both hands off the wheels of life while climbing upward and devote my life to helping people. You want to know what's crazy? The more I helped people, the higher I went up the ladder! I became more successful when it was about THEM and not ME! I must tell you this: I may never make it all the way to the top, but I will go far, and I'll be surrounded by individuals whom I have uplifted and love. I hope to springboard friends higher than myself, these friends I call Goal Diggers.

Stop thinking about yourself so much and start thinking about others as well. Maybe you can't take both hands off the ladder of life but at least use one hand! One day you will be able to hit cruise control and use both hands to help. That is the way I live my life. How do you live yours?

A Few Million-Dollar Ideas

You may have heard the statement "Ideas rule the world." The forces of nature respond to the implementation of ideas. Whatever you see around you today, science and technological innovations, political and economic advances, great business successes, they are all a product of an idea in someone's mind that came to fruition. Every business you see being successful today was once an idea in the mind of its founder.

The first step to having a successful business is having a good business idea; what do you want to do? Most businesses have failed either because they were not based on ideas that the society needed, or action on the ideas was not well planned and executed. Lack of the right business idea or inability to properly execute it may be most aspiring entrepreneurs' nightmare. Until you discover that million-dollar idea, you will continue to be a struggling entrepreneur.

Are you ready for the million-dollar business idea that will transform your life and set you on the path of massive financial success? Then you should read the next few paragraphs with close attention. I am about to show you an easy and sure path to entrepreneurial success.

What about having a splendid idea and being clueless as to how to execute it? I understand that feeling. You know your idea can lead to great business success, but you don't even know the next step to take. In some cases, you believe you know what to do and set out to do it, but at some point you are stopped, totally bereft of forward-moving ideas. I have been there before, and I have conquered that battle countless times.

What you need is a platform, a home, a community of business ideas and executioners that will help you develop your own business ideas and, most importantly, give you million-dollar business ideas and help you fund it.

I have created eleven businesses, and of those eleven, three have failed and eight have become successful businesses over the past nine years of my entrepreneurship journey. I have also sold three of the eight. I used to undertake an average of 10-12 speaking engagements per month, in different countries around the world. This year I decided that my three-year-old and my wife are more important to me, so I reduced my motivational speaking engagements to 3-4 per month. Still, my mind never stops working. I keep getting new great business ideas. I have a great many well-documented business ideas just waiting for somebody willing to execute them. But I understand that I have to focus at this point in my life.

This is why I decided to write this book, to help as many people as I can to start their business and help them achieve their entrepreneurship dreams. I have also decided to give out my well-documented business ideas to serious aspiring entrepreneurs to execute for free, along with a detailed guide on how to start, execute, and scale, plus free consultancy.

I also thought it would be great to have a platform where entrepreneurs can get help on starting, executing, and scaling their businesses. This is a website providing access to a pool of regular materials and consultancy, a typical business community, a world of business innovations and ideas. This is all you need to transform your life and guarantee your financial success.

You are already thinking, how on earth is all this going to work? Well, it's just a click away, go to www.StartSuccessHere.com/NOW. On that page I'll give you a free video with three business ideas worth a million dollars in revenue each! This is just as small sampling of what you'll get by being a part of our community.

Visit www.StartSuccessHere.com/NOW to open yourself to a world of business success and ideas.

ABOUT THE AUTHOR
ELIJAH DESMOND

Elijah Desmond is a serial entrepreneur who speaks worldwide in up to three to four cities per month. He has presented more than seven hundred hours since 2009. After graduating from Ohio State University, he moved to Honolulu, Hawaii, where he started his first of eleven businesses. He is known for having fun-filled, engaging presentations and integrating motivational speaking into all of his events. Mr. Desmond is a dynamic professional speaker who combines fun and education through his experience coaching more than four hundred professional teams nationwide. Elijah now resides in South Florida with his wife and 4-year-old daughter.

Made in the USA
Monee, IL
18 February 2022